نُشرت للمرة الأولى من قِبل سيكرت غواي ميديا المحدودة ٢٠١٥

حُقوق النشر السيدة غيل دالدي ٢٠١٣

جميع الحقوق محفوظة. لا يُسمح بإعادة إنتاج أي جزء من هذا الكتاب بأي شكل او طريقة سواء كانت بيانية ام الكترونية، من دون الرُخصة الخطية المُسبَقة للناشر.

الأشياء التي تَحدُث من قِبل الصُدفة   -   ISBN ٥-٥-٩٩٤٧٩٥٧-٠-٩٧٨

سلسلة كُتُب تعلّم من جانس : لطلب نُسخة من الكتاب أرسل بريد الكتروني orders@learnbychancebooks.com
او اتصِل ١-٦٠٤-٩٤٧-٩٢٨٣

زورونا على الانترنت على www.learnbychancebooks.com

المُخرج المُبدع: جيسون بامفورد – تصميم بامفورد www.bamforddesign.com

تصوير: غيل دالدي

مستشار الإبداعية : فلورا نوايى – florangraphic@gmail.com

ترجمة: شهله سلطان

شُكر خاص لمارك جونستون على مُساعدتهِ.

جانس هو اسم ابني، ولكنه يعني أيضا ... أن الصور تم التقاطها عن طريق الصدفة.

الطبعة : عربي - انكليزي

نُشِرت من قِبل:
سيكرت غواي ميديا المحدودة
صندوق ٩١١٩٤
غرب فانكوفر، كولومبيا البريطانية، كندا
٦N٧VV

www.secretquaymedia.com

طُبِعت في الولايات المتحدة الأمريكية

First published by Secret Quay Media. 2015

Copyright © M. Gail Daldy 2013 - 2017

All rights reserved. No part of this publication may be reproduced in any form or means, graphic, electronic, without the prior written permission of the publisher.

Things That Happen By Chance | ISBN 978-0-9947957-5-5

Learn By Chance book series: To order a copy of the book email orders@learnbychancebooks.com or call 1-604-947-9283

Visit us online at www.learnbychancebooks.com

Creative Director: Jason Bamford – Bamford Design – www.bamforddesign.com

Photographs by: Gail Daldy

Creative Consultant: Flora Navaee – florangraphic@gmail.com

Arabic Translation: Shahla Sultan

A special thank you to all of those who contributed to the translation and, to Mark Johnston for all of his help.

A note on this translation: "Chance" is the name of my son, but it also means that........... the pictures were taken by chance.

Arabic/English edition

Published by:
Secret Quay Media Inc.
Box 91194
West Vancouver, BC, Canada
V7V 3N6

www.secretquaymedia.com

Printed in the USA

ما حدث بالصُدفة

عِندما انظُر الى بعض الصور الفوتوغرافية لابننا وهو يكبر أعودُ بالذاكرة الى طفولته المُبكرة. فَكرت انه من الممتع ان أضع مجموعة من هذه اللقطات الخاصة داخل كتاب صغير، كهدية له بمناسبة تخرجهُ من الثانوية.

نمط الحروف المطبوعة في الحقيقة مُكون من بعض أولى كِتاباته الخطية في المدرسة الابتدائية. كان أملي ان يتمكن من استذكار طفولته وبعض اللحظات المميزة ومشاركة دروس حياته اليومية التي تعلمها عندما كان طفلا. تلك اللحظات في النهاية هي التي صَنعت منه الرجل الناضج الذي هو عليه اليوم.

نأمل ان تستمتع بقراءة الكتاب مع قُرّائِك الصغار والتكلم بفرح حول الأشياء البسيطة في الحياة التي علمتهم دروس كثيرة.

شكر خاص
أود أن اشكر والداي لجعلي واعية لهذه الأشياء الصغيرة في الحياة

What Happened By Chance

While looking through some photographs of our son Chance growing up they instantly took me back in time to his early childhood. As my gift to him upon graduating high school I thought it would be fun to put together a collection of these chance snapshots into a little book.

The type face is actually created from some of his earliest hand writing in primary school. My hope was that he would be able to reflect back on his childhood and some of the special moments and share these everyday life lessons that he had learned as a child with his own children. It was these moments after all that made him into the person he has grown up to be.

Hopefully you can enjoy the book with your own little readers and with a smile talk about the simple things in life that teach them so much.

A Special Thanks
I'd like to thank my parents for making me aware of these little things in life.

www.learnbychancebooks.com

الى جانس:

رؤيتك وأنت تصبح الشخص الذي أنت عليه اليوم أعطاني متعة الأمومة القصوى.

To Chance:

For affording me a mother's ultimate pleasure of watching you become **you**.

الأشياء التي تحدُث من قبل الصُدفة

Things That Happen By Chance

مُشاركة دروس الحياة البسيطة مع الأطفال في كل مكان

Sharing simple life lessons with children everywhere

الحياة مليئة بالمفاجآت
الصغيرة دائماً

Life is always filled
with little surprises

عندما تَطلب شيئاً ما
تذكر دائماً أن تقول
من فضلِك

When you are asking
for something always
remember to say please

عندما يُساعدك احد ما تذكر دائماً أن تبتسم وتقول شكراً

When someone helps you always remember to smile and say thank you

إذا مضغت العلكة تذكر ٣ أشياء:
١. لا تُخرجها من فمك
٢. لا تبتلعها
٣. لا تضعها في شعرك أبداً

If you chew gum
remember 3 things:
1. Keep it in your mouth
2. Don't swallow it
3. Never put it in your hair

ضع خطة للشُروع بعملك فان ذلك سيُساعدك على انجازه

When there is a job to be done it helps to plan your attack

والتزم بها

And stick to it

حتى النهاية

Until the very end

15

كلا لا أعتقد أنني أكلتُ أي قِطعة جُبْن

NO I don't think
I ate any cheesies

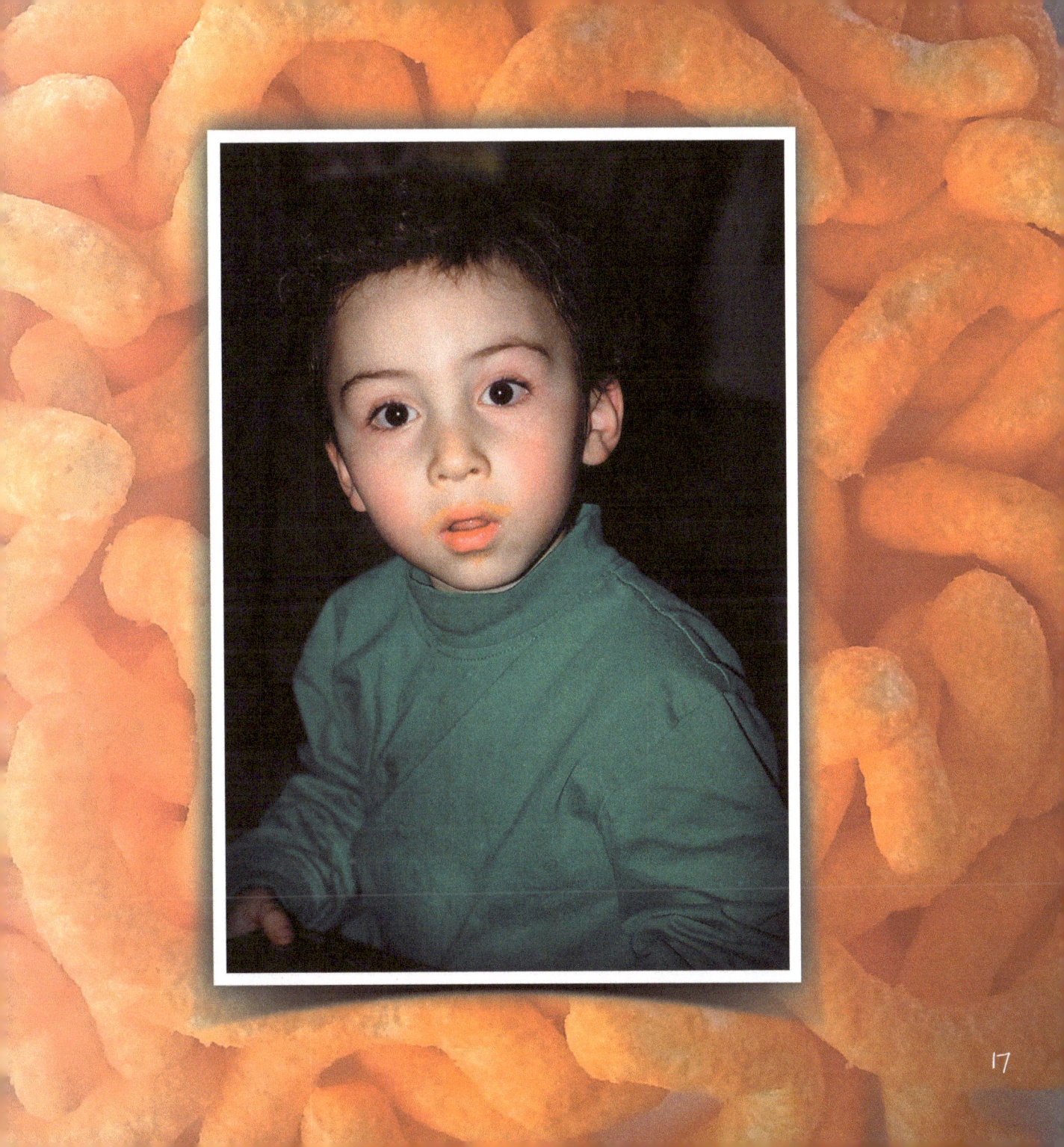

إطعام الطيور والبط
أمر مُمتِع جِداً

Feeding the birds and ducks is lots of fun

لكن لا تنسى أن
تُغلِق البوابة

But don't forget
to close gate

باستِطاعتك أن تأكل
الكثير من كعك الشوكولاتة

you can eat too
much chocolate cake

احرص على أن تفرش أسنانك كل يوم للحِفاظ على نظافتِهم وصحتِهم

Be sure to brush your teeth everyday to keep them clean and healthy

لا تُدخِل أصابعك
في انفك أبداً

Always keep your
fingers on the outside
of your nose

إذا شككتَ بشيء ما

If there is something
you are not sure about

شخص او شيء ما جعلك تشعر بعدم الراحة في داخلك احرص على إبلاغ شخص بالغ في الحال

And someone or something makes you feel not right inside be sure to tell a grownup right away

إذا أردت أن تخرجَ ريحاً من تحتك فافعل ذلك لوحدك

Wind and thunder from down under should be done in private

أنا أسف فقد كان ذلك حادثاً عرضياً

I'm sorry it was an accident

تَعلُم عمل البسكويت أمر مُمتِع

It's fun learning how to bake cookies

احرص على مزج جميع المُكونات مع بعضها جيداً

Make sure you mix all of the ingredients together really good

تذكر أن تغسل يداك دائماً قبل أن تبدأ

And always remember to wash your hands before you start

عندما يَحتاج أحد أصدقائك
شخصاً ما ليتحدث إليهِ

When a friend needs
someone to talk to

حاول دائماً أن تكون مستمعاً جيداً

Always try to be
a good listener

إياك أن تأكُل الثلج
الذي لونهُ أصفر

Never never ever ever
eat yellow snow

يقول الناس أحياناً
أشياء غير صحيحة

Sometimes people tell
stories that are not true

احرص على قَولك
أشياء صحيحة

Make sure you tell
stories that are true

من المُمتع أن تشعُر بالرياح وهي تداعب شعرك

It's fun to feel the wind blow through your hair

والرمال تَتلوى بين
أصابع قدميك

and the sand wiggle
between your toes

كونك لطيفاً يجلب لك
جميع أنواع الأصدقاء

Being nice makes
all kind of friends

عِندما تُغني غني
من أعماق قلبك

When you sing sing
with all your heart

أُرقص حينما تسنح
لك الفرصة

Whenever you get
the chance just dance

أعطي لنفسك الوقت دائماً
للتوقف وشم الأزهار

Always take the time to
stop and smell the flowers

أشكُرك على قِراءة كتابي الصغير والسماحَ لي بمشاركتكَ بعض دُروس حياتي الواقعية من الصُدفة

Thank you for reading my little book and letting me share some of my real life lessons with you by chance

حول الكاتب

ولدَت غيل دالدي في جيليواك، كولومبيا البريطانية على الساحل الغربي لكندا ثم استقرت في جزيرة بوين التي تقع بعيداً عن جزيرة فانكوفر. كأي شابة فقد سافرت على نطاق واسع لتجربة الثقافات المختلفة والحياة اليومية في العديد من البلدان.

أدركَتْ خلال هذه التجربة إن الأطفال مُتشابهون في جميع أنحاء العالم ويُمكنهم التعلم من بعضهم البعض ومن الأشياء البسيطة المحيطة بهم. إنها تؤمن بان مجموعة جانس للصور الفوتوغرافية تُصور العديد من دُروس الحياة اليومية وتوضِحها بطريقة سهلة الفهم.

About the Author

Gail Daldy was born in Chilliwack, British Columbia on the west coast of Canada before settling on Bowen Island which is just off the Vancouver mainland. As a young woman she travelled extensively experiencing different cultures and everyday living in numerous countries.

From this she realized children are similar the world over and can learn from each other and the simple things that surround them. She believes this collection of chance photographs captures many of these everyday life lessons and illustrates them in an easy to understand way.

هذا الكتاب الأول لسلسلة التعلُم بالصُدفة

This is the first book of the Learn by Chance series.

"Kids will really relate to the photos in this book and be both inspired and amused." - **Temple Grandin - Author, Thinking in Pictures**

"These masterful photographs with entertaining and clever text makes " Things That Happen By Chance " a perfect book to impart useful knowledge to a young child and start wonderful conversations."
- **Tom Best - Executive Director, First Book Canada**

"A delightful addition to our Reach Out and Read program!" - **Dr. Laurie Green**

Things That Happen By Chance

To Say "A picture is worth 1000 words" seems so cliché while at the same time appropriate in pointing out the obvious in this little book of Chance.

As seen through the eyes of one little boy a growing visual interactive experience of a child learning simple life lessons that can be shared with children all over the world.

Seeing and reading about his adventures as they happen creates a great conversation opener for parents giving them an opportunity to talk about similar enjoyable moments and lessons learned with their own children.

Gail Daldy

Taking a closer look at the little things in life

learnbychancebooks.com

ISBN 978-0-9947957-5-5

$18.95 USD | for ages 2 & up

ISBN 978-0-9947957-5-5
COPYRIGHT 2013 - 2017 © Secret Quay Media Inc. | All Rights Reserved | Printed in the USA

www.ingramcontent.com/pod-product-compliance
Lightning Source LLC
Chambersburg PA
CBHW061930290426
44113CB00024B/2864